DEVOTIONAL FOR BLACK MEN

50 Devotions for African American Men. Offers Unique Insight Into How You Can Deepen Your Personal Relationship With Christ.

Annett Hill

Know Your Identity and Worth in Christ. Experience the Love of God Through His Words. Believe What He Says About You.

TABLE OF CONTENTS

INTRODUCTION

Why This Devotional is for Black Men

As the aroma of jasmine tea filled the room, I sat with my Bible, accompanied by a cherished photo of my husband, Noris, and our son, Martin. In that moment, I felt the weight of the world my Black men navigate. The unseen burdens, and the societal pressures, are all too familiar.

That's why I penned this devotional. As a Black woman, I've witnessed firsthand the resilience and strength exhibited by Black men like Noris and Martin. This book is my gift to them, a tool to deepen their relationship with Jesus Christ.

While the world may define Black men by their struggles, Jesus sees them differently. He sees them as His beloved children, created in His image, endowed with limitless potential. This 50-day devotional serves as a roadmap to strengthen that bond with Christ. Life's chaos can be overwhelming, but these daily readings offer bite-sized wisdom to nourish the spirit.

Most importantly, this devotional makes faith accessible. Each entry includes a scripture verse, a practical application, and a prayer tool for busy schedules and hectic lives.

Black man, you are a son of God, equipped to overcome any challenge. Let's journey together along this path of faith and empowerment.

DAY 1

"But I say unto you, love your enemies, bless them that curse you, do good to them that hate you, and pray for them which despitefully use you, and persecute you."
Matthew 5:44.

The world seems to be reeling under the weight of racism. You might be the victim of such hatred. That's because they recognize greatness in you. Consider why Jesus was hated, because he was great and popular among people everywhere he went, and he was admired.

But it is what you do with those feelings that will be the true test of your humanity. Hatred is a feeling that will consume you. It develops more hatred, anger, and soon or later violence.

Love comes from the inside. It is how much you have grown in loving and appreciating yourself that will make you appreciate and love others. You were born with love in your heart. Hate is learned, and it takes effort to hate.

God, I pray you would heal the spiritual, emotional, and physical wounds many of us black men carry for the color of our skin. Remove the spirit of division at the root of racism and replace it with your love. Amen.

Lord guide me.

_____
_____
_____
_____
_____
_____
_____
_____
_____
_____

Lord Teach me to:

_____
_____
_____
_____
_____
_____
_____
_____
_____

Today I am thankful for:

_____
_____
_____
_____
_____
_____
_____

IDENTITY IN GOD

Day 2

"For you died, and your life is now hidden with Christ in God. When Christ, who is your life, appears, then you also will appear with him in glory."
Colossians 3:3-4.

Several black men have been called names they don't bear, and over time, they unconsciously accept the wrong identity given them by society. Remove the stigma and opinions of others, so you can be whom God created you to be.

Nevertheless, no longer will you accept that you are a liar, a troublemaker, a deviant, a rapist, and what have you. Your identity is in God. The scripture says, "your life hides in Christ with God." This simply means you're whom God says you are.

You're the head, you're prosperous, you're sitting by his side in heavenly places, you are not a slave, but a son, and if a son, then an heir. Your identity is in God, not your skin color.

Dear God, my identity lies in you. My identity is light in place of darkness. I ask my identity in you overwhelm and overshadow me, so that I would no longer yield to the misconception society has about my color and race. Instead, I will know that only your words towards my life, future, and destiny are the truth. Amen.

Lord guide me.

_____
_____
_____
_____
_____
_____
_____
_____
_____
_____

Lord Teach me to:

_____
_____
_____
_____
_____
_____
_____
_____
_____

Today I am thankful for:

_____
_____
_____
_____
_____
_____
_____
_____

THE PROMISE OF ETERNAL LIFE

Day 3

And this is the testimony: God has given us eternal life, and this life is in his Son. Whoever has the Son has life; whoever does not have the Son of God does not have life.
1 John 5:11-12.

Our culture is obsessive about longevity. Although it's natural to desire many healthy years on earth, you must remind yourself that life doesn't end with physical death. The bigger issue is eternal destiny.

There is only one way to assure that you are destined for a life in heaven. You must recognize your hopeless, sinful condition, turn to Jesus Christ in faith, and receive forgiveness of sins and the gift of eternal life.

Reaching a healthy old age is a worthy goal, but nothing more important than receiving the Savior and the gift of eternity in His presence.

Heavenly Father, thank You for the glorious gospel of grace and the truth it contains. Thank You that I have life in Him by grace and trust in His shed blood at Calvary. How I praise Your name that I have received eternal life and that nothing can ever separate me. Amen.

Lord guide me.

Lord Teach me to:

Today I am thankful for:

Day 4

Ah, Lord God! Behold, You have made the heavens and the earth by Your great power and by Your outstretched arm! Nothing is too difficult for you.
Jeremiah 32:17.

Every man is created in the image of God, regardless of his skin color. For this reason, the Scripture says, "Let us make man in our image." Therefore, you must think the way God thinks.

You have to look inward, recognize God in His creation, and value each other as a black man, because you are made for His glory, and nothing less.

To truly understand the reflection of your God in His creation and to know His will for your life, we must know who the Creator Himself really is by placing your faith in Him.

Dear God, beautiful are your works, outstanding are your deeds. I affirm today that I am created in your image and for your glory; I see you in me. I reflect and radiate your beauty. By your grace, I wouldn't think less of myself with my skin color. I am a black man, and I am created after the order of God. Amen.

Lord guide me.

Lord Teach me to:

Today I am thankful for:

Day 5

The Lord is my rock, my fortress, and my deliverer; my God, my strength, in whom I will trust; my buckler, and the horn of my salvation, and my high tower.
Psalm 18:2.

The Psalmist says that the Lord is my strength. This isn't an understatement, but affirms how confident you are when you rely on or put your trust in the Lord.

When there are different reasons to be anxious, worried, perplexed, and moody, why don't you commit it to God? When you hand over all to him, he takes over, and when he takes over, your joy knows no bounds.

I know that you have many expectations as a man, as a son, as a father, and much more. Why don't you hand over to the greatest man who ever lived and let him take the wheel, while you watch with rejoicing?

Awesome God, I am glad I'm yours. I'm filled with several expectations and demands. I understand fully now that I can't do it on my own. My strength is little, dear God. I look up to you, help me trust in you, and help me rely on you, because it's only in you that the full joy and happiness that I seek and desire lives. Amen.

Lord guide me.

Lord Teach me to:

Today I am thankful for:

CAST YOUR CARES ON GOD

Day 6

Cast your cares on the Lord, and he will sustain you; He will never let the righteous be shaken.
Psalm 55:22.

God is not a man who will lie, nor is he a son of a man who will repent. He sincerely cares for you. Your worries are his worries. He wants you to be better and be the things you want to become, but you know what, you have to cast your cares on him.

Obviously, you have several bills to pay, several problems and challenges, from society to marital, career, family, and several others. But it's not over until God says so.

Who says you cannot overcome as a black man? Who says you can't survive because you're black? All you need to do is cast your cares on your creator. He created you as a black man, and he is ready to help you throughout the journey.

Almighty God, the one who cares for me, I cast all my burdens, worries, and anxieties unto you today. Please take charge. In areas where I haven't allowed you to rule and reign as you ought to, forgive me, oh God, take over, rule and reign mightily. Subdue every battle and let your name alone be glorified. Amen.

Lord guide me.

Lord Teach me to:

Today I am thankful for:

Day 7

And the peace of God, which transcends all understanding,
will guard your hearts and minds in Christ Jesus.
Philippians 4:7.

Jesus is the prince of peace. When he is the anchor of a man's life, there is nothing to worry about. There'd be trying times, but his peace will keep one's heart in order and at rest. Nobody can steal your peace unless you allow them to.

Peace is not in the government, it is not in a satisfactory job, nor in wife or children, and the true and most efficient peace lies with God. His peace is clear even amid an outraging and bewildering storm. Choose to believe God's promises, keep your eyes on Jesus to find peace.

Receiving inner peace is a gift of the Holy Spirit and comes to you when you are at your weakest when you stop relying on your own strength and allow God to work in you.

Oh, God of peace, as a man, several challenges that compete with both my inner and outer peace. I ask you to fill my life with your peace. I don't want to live in fear anymore, but I want to live a peaceful life. Fill my heart with your peace that transcends all human understanding. Amen.

Lord guide me.

_____
_____
_____
_____
_____
_____
_____
_____
_____
_____

Lord Teach me to:

_____
_____
_____
_____
_____
_____
_____
_____
_____

Today I am thankful for:

_____
_____
_____
_____
_____
_____
_____
_____

LET GOD BE YOUR HOPE

Day 8

But those who hope in the Lord will renew their strength.
They will soar on wings like eagles; they will run and not
grow weary, they will walk and not be faint.
Isaiah 40:31.

The Scripture says, "I will not cut the earnest expectation of the righteous short." Proverbs 23:17-18. I know that you are hopeful, you have several expectations, and you want to make several life-changing decisions as a black man. Let God be your hope.

Spend time with the Word. Romans 15:4 says the Bible was written to give us encouragement and hope. The Psalms can be particularly helpful in difficult times because they express the real feelings of the writers and give comfort.

In those moments when you are filled with doubt, when fear and uncertainty plague your thoughts and actions, read this scripture to hold on to peace and security. Jeremiah 29:11. Rely on the faithfulness of the Lord. Trusting Him will always turn out for your good.

God, you are the hope of the hopeless. Oh, God, I don't want to put my hopes in my country or in my family, nation, government or what have you. Jesus, help me hope in You. Oh, God, constantly and continuously cast my gaze on You. Amen.

Lord guide me.

Lord Teach me to:

Today I am thankful for:

THE JOY OF THE LORD IS YOUR STRENGTH

Day 9

"These things have I spoken unto you, that my joy might remain in you, and that your joy might be full."
John 15:11.

◆◇◆

There is an office of strength in God, he fills you with irresistible strength, and how this happens is through the fulfillment of His joy. If the joy of the Lord is in you, there is no weariness.

You do the impossible with ease, because his joy is the fuel needed for strength. He strengthens a man by filling such a man with joy, the joy unspeakable and inexplicable. He wants to fill you with strength for the journey; simply accept his overflowing joy.

The strength God gives you is His grace. The joy of the Lord is your strength, which is brought to fullness when you accept His provision of righteousness through grace, which reconciles you so that you can enjoy His presence.

Dear Lord, the stereotyped black man is usually saddened and burdened, courtesy of various worries, obstructions and barricades. Let your joy take the full course of my life; break every wall of sadness and unhappiness. Destroy every cycle of weakness, weariness and fear. I refuse to be part of the unhappy generation. My going out and coming in are filled with unusual rejoicing. Amen.

Lord guide me.

Lord Teach me to:

Today I am thankful for:

Day 10

For we are His workmanship, created in Christ Jesus for works, which God prepared beforehand that we should walk in them.
Ephesians 2:10.

The devil and his agents continue to feed you with the lies that you are nothing and will not equal anything in life, especially because you are a black man.

Don't believe the lie, he starts from the color of your skin; he reminds you of several black men who don't have their lives all settled. You must respond with courage that Christ came to this sinful world for you.

More so, God, in His infinite mercy and loving-kindness, had explicitly stated, confirmed, and established that his thoughts for you are good and not evil, in order to give you an expected end even before you were conceived. How loving.

Dear God, thank you, because your thoughts towards me are of good and not evil to give me a glorious end. Oh, God, I pray that I will not surrender to the lie of the devil. Rather, I will trust you. I will rest in your overflowing grace and know that I am a work in progress. Amen.

Lord guide me.

Lord Teach me to:

Today I am thankful for:

21

WALK BY FAITH

Day 11

And without faith, it is impossible to please Him, for he who comes to God must believe He is, and He is a rewarder of those who seek Him.
Hebrews 11:6.

Through faith, you can please God, because there are several unimaginable things He wants to do in you. Without faith, doubt creeps in. Galatians 2:16 know that a person is not justified by the works of the law, but by faith in Jesus Christ.

You may ask me, a black man? Yes, you. You are His creation, and He will do amazing things with you, but if doubt creeps in, God can't do much. The Scripture says a double-minded man is unstable in all his ways. James 1:8.

Our path as Christians should be identifiably different from one who does not believe and has been saved by grace. Jesus calls you his friend, and you are called to live your life close to him, confident and worshiping.

Dear God, sometimes my faith is weak, I can't trust in you as I ought to. Help me, oh God, help my weak faith, help me not to be double-minded, but have a strong faith in you with all my heart. I desire to please you, but I can't on my own. Amen.

Lord guide me.

Lord Teach me to:

Today I am thankful for:

LET GO AND LET GOD

Day 12

Do not be anxious about anything, but in every situation, by prayer and petition, with thanksgiving, present your requests to God.
Philippians 4:6.

Let go and let God be the best option you can make as a black man. Why? It saves time and energy. You hold on to past hurts and hatred from society, you are angry at too many things, but you have to let go of them all and let God take control.

Give God a chance, let go of malice, and let go of the unforgiving spirit. Throw it all at the feet of Jesus. When your hands are weak and tired, God's hands are strong and powerful!

Surrendering to God means literally giving up. It says to God that you are not enough to deal with your worries, and He must take over. When you finally let go, you give God space to wield His mighty arm in your life.

Lord, Society has called me several names that I know do not belong to me. It aches my heart, but today I let you into all my affairs. Those things that I held on to and have allowed me to remain in one spot, the pains, the unforgiveness, the emotional injuries I'm unconsciously harbored inside. Take charge of it. Amen.

Lord guide me.

_____
_____
_____
_____
_____
_____
_____
_____
_____
_____

Lord Teach me to:

_____
_____
_____
_____
_____
_____
_____
_____

Today I am thankful for:

_____
_____
_____
_____
_____
_____
_____
_____

25

Day 13

For it is by grace you have been saved, through faith, and this is not from yourselves, it is the gift of God.
Ephesians 2:8.

As a black man, you could not have saved yourself. Your righteous works could not have saved you either. To be saved by grace means you have received a gift from God that you do not deserve. The grace of God gave you what you lacked: righteousness.

There is no height a black man achieves in life, that he will save himself, none. You found only the power to save in God. Money does not save, jobs do not save, children do not save. What saves is God and God alone.

He is ready to save you, if only you open up to him, to save you from attacks, darkness, pandemonium, disasters, and everything. Grace alone means that God loves, forgives, and saves you, not because of who you are or what you do, but because of the work of Christ.

Dear God, my Savior, please save me, save me from the distress of a black man, save me from the anguish posed at the black man every second. Save me by your grace, because whoever the son of man sets free; is free indeed. Amen.

Lord guide me.

Lord Teach me to:

Today I am thankful for:

27

Day 14

Keep this Book of the Law always on your lips; meditate on it day and night, so that you may be careful to do everything written in it. Then you will be prosperous and successful.
Joshua 1:8.

The only path to success is to meditate and to dwell on the Word of God. Especially in an environment where the chances of a black man to succeed are slim, because of his skin color amidst many others, but God is the giver of success.

God is the path to real success. If society says no to your success as a black man, and God says yes, no man can stop such success. Jesus must be the foundation of everything you do.

Your priority from henceforth should be in the word of God because through his word, outstanding success is guaranteed. He provides all we need and guides us in the direction we are to go.

Dear Lord, regardless of how much I try, society reminds me of my skin pigmentation, and it's like an obstruction for me in doing great things. Help me sit with your word, help me know your word, and help me do your word, oh God, thereby achieving true success. Amen.

Lord guide me.

Lord Teach me to:

Today I am thankful for:

Day 15

Peace I leave with you; my peace, I give you. I do not give to you as the world gives. Do not let your hearts be troubled, and do not be afraid.
John 14:27.

◆◇◆

Being worrisome in today's society is like a normal phenomenon that goes hand in hand with life. Especially for a black man, there are too many things to worry about, but here God says, "Worry no more."

It seems obscure and impossible, because every new day comes with a new thing to worry about. Regardless, the one who knows all things has told you directly without mincing words that "worry not."

You just have to believe in God and push on. Clearly, what you see may not reflect, "worry not," but remember the just will live by faith and not by sight. So "worry not," hold on to God, and you will certainly share your testimony.

Dear God, I don't want to worry, I'm worried not because I want to, I worry when I don't know the outcome of a situation. Today, I surrender all my worries to you; I choose not to worry, in the place of worry; I will believe your word and hold on to it. Amen.

Lord guide me.

_____
_____
_____
_____
_____
_____
_____
_____
_____
_____

Lord Teach me to:

_____
_____
_____
_____
_____
_____
_____
_____

Today I am thankful for:

_____
_____
_____
_____
_____
_____
_____
_____

PRAY WITHOUT CEASING

Day 16

Rejoice always. Pray without ceasing. In everything, give thanks; for this is the will of God in Christ Jesus for you. 1 Thessalonian 5:16-18.

In the midst of several denigrations and despicable acts, praying is a sure remedy for a black man to counteract the effects of these denigrations. The Scriptures record that "men should pray and not faint." Continuous conversations with your heavenly Father are one of the means He uses to personally guide you.

As a black man with several mental images of fear, attacks, and evil, prayer must be your watchword. Prayer has changed things. If you seek the Lord and spend time regularly in His Word, you will be transformed.

Prayer invites God to do His work in you. Although you cannot change a single divine plan or make the Lord change His mind, you can invite him to change you. In prayer, you submit to God's will, repent of sin, and ask Him to form you into the image of His Son.

Dear God, strengthen me to pray, help me tarry in prayer. Help me not be weary or waver. Oh, Lord, I regard you as my only confidant with whom I share my pain, happiness and testimony. Amen.

Lord guide me.

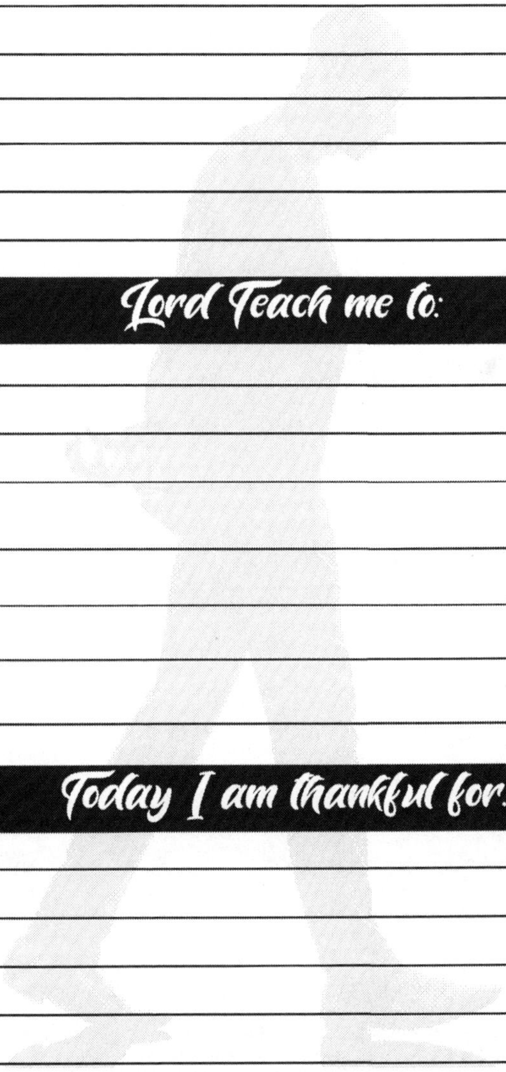

(blank lined writing area)

Lord Teach me to:

(blank lined writing area)

Today I am thankful for:

(blank lined writing area)

DIRECT YOUR PATH

Day 17

"Trust in the Lord with all your heart and lean not on your own understanding, in all your ways, acknowledge him, and he will direct your path."
Proverbs 3:5.

Men are most often coupled and trusted with the responsibility to make certain decisions. And if such decisions are fruitful, it is worth the man's credit. If not fruitful, trust in such a man could be withdrawn.

Too many people trust you in making healthy decisions. Who will you trust? Responsibilities continue to draw your attention; trust God completely to lead your path.

Part of acknowledging God is by trusting in Him. This means you cannot trust in yourself. The world advocates the necessity to trust in yourself, not in God. As a believer, you know that your trust must be in God alone. Christians cannot trust in anything or anyone else.

God, the road seems clouded and bleak. Several responsibilities keep calling my name. Help me, oh Lord, you know all things; I surrender all to you, lead me according to your loving-kindness, oh Lord, and establish the works of my hands. Amen.

Lord guide me.

Lord Teach me to:

Today I am thankful for:

Day 18

"Be very careful, then, how you live, not as unwise but as wise, making the most of every opportunity because the days are evil. Therefore, do not be foolish, but understand what the Lord's will is."
Ephesians 5:15-17.

It is absolute ignorance and sheer foolishness to live life without wisdom from the Supreme Being. Only God can give you wisdom to live life. It is only the wisdom of God that can establish you as a man.

As a black man, you must understand what the will of the Lord is for you every time and every season. When a man lives through the wisdom of the Lord, he appears to his other folks as an unusual personality.

Without the disclosure of the spiritual truths of God by the Holy Spirit, human wisdom remains of no value. The Lord knows all human plans; He knows that they are futile. Psalm 94:11.

I pray, oh God, for your wisdom, let the fount of your wisdom rest upon me. Fill me up with your wisdom. Let each of my steps and decisions rule and mark by your wisdom. Amen.

Lord guide me.

Lord Teach me to:

Today I am thankful for:

PURPOSE TO LIVE AN OUTSTANDING LIFE

Day 19

"For we are God's handiwork, created in Christ Jesus to do good works, which God prepared in advance for us to do."
Ephesians 2:10.

As a black man, there is an outstanding life God has prepared for you, and it is when you fully grasp the details of your purpose that you can live an outstanding life. Good works include sharing the gospel in everything we do.

God always had you in mind, regardless of the usual stereotype associated with a black man. More reason, he said, you are God's handiwork created to do good work in Christ Jesus.

We want to be a place that heals as we help to build homes and tear down walls of racial division. It is about the good works that God has given us to do. These good works require God's grace. Good works reflect the ministry of Christ, and these good works fulfill the mission of Christ.

Oh, God, I know you have created me for a purpose; I pray I established the purpose for which you have created me, and it comes to fulfillment. In your infinite mercy, let nothing obstruct or hinder me from fulfilling my purpose in life and destiny. Amen.

Lord guide me.

_____
_____
_____
_____
_____
_____
_____
_____
_____

Lord Teach me to:

_____
_____
_____
_____
_____
_____
_____
_____

Today I am thankful for:

_____
_____
_____
_____
_____
_____
_____
_____

Day 20

"Don't be afraid, for I am with you." Don't be discouraged,
for I am your God. I will strengthen you and help you.
I will hold you up with my victorious right hand."
Isaiah 41:10.

Sometimes life struggles can be outrageous, and deep in you, you are looking for a way to escape. A way to circumvent the challenges, the bills to be paid, the problems associated with the identity of a black man, and much more.

He said there is strength to overcome every battle. One of the most important ways to overcome a battle is to know God's promises about you and remind him of his promises written to you. These are his words for you. "I will help you, don't be afraid."

God calls and commands us not to be afraid. When we let fear take over, we take our eyes off Him and His promises. As we can see above, God gives us five reasons in a passage of Scripture alone.

Dear Lord, now I know that there's strength available to overcome the battles of life, and the strength lives in you. Strengthen me, oh God, to overcome the challenges and battles of life. Amen.

Lord guide me.

Lord Teach me to:

Today I am thankful for:

Day 21

"For the Lord shall supply all your needs according to his riches in glory by Christ Jesus."
Philippians 4:19.

God still provides for His own, and when I say His own, you as a black man are His own, because you are His creation, and he holds you in high esteem. I appreciate this part in Scripture most. We may not always get our desires, but in Christ Jesus, we can be sure that God faithfully fulfills all our needs.

When we say his riches in glory, we simply say more than abundance. This is because God has everything you need in enormous quantities, and he has promised he will meet your needs. It may not seem like it, but that's what it is.

He will definitely reach you with his outstretched arm, and he will meet your needs. And more importantly, he will never fail or leave you! Hardships are opportunities to trust and know the Creator. Fortunately, we serve a great God who always provides in dark times of life.

Dear God, my needs are many. My lack and desire seem to overwhelm me, but I trust in your provisional power. You are rich in wealth and prosperity. God, in your infinite mercy, fulfill all my needs. Amen.

Lord guide me.

Lord Teach me to:

Today I am thankful for:

LIVE A HUMBLE LIFE, NOT OF SERVITUDE

"Humble yourselves, therefore, under God's mighty hand, that he may lift you up in due time."
1 Peter 5:6.

God called you to humility as a black man, and not to servitude. I understand well that people in your environment might want to turn your humble nature into servitude, but you must understand that it is a humble life to which God has called you, not servitude.

Humble simply means not high or lofty, unpretentious, while servitude means slavery. You are not a slave to anyone; you are God's Son and heir. Let us be humble before our Creator for the gift of life we have been given.

The importance of humility is directly linked to the deadly consequences of pride. Pride separates us from God, because we do not acknowledge and appreciate the eternal sovereignty of our Lord.

Dear Lord, due to past antecedents, as much as I desire to be humble, I'm scared they will take me for granted. It's clearer to me now that humility was one characteristic you exhibited while on earth. I ask for grace and strength to live a life of humility. Amen.

Lord guide me.

_____
_____
_____
_____
_____
_____
_____
_____
_____
_____

Lord Teach me to:

_____
_____
_____
_____
_____
_____
_____
_____
_____
_____

Today I am thankful for:

_____
_____
_____
_____
_____
_____
_____
_____

Day 23

God showed how much he loved us by sending his one and only Son into the world so that we might have eternal life through him.
1 John 4:9.

Everyone wants to be loved. But human devotion is not always reliable. Even the most stable relationships change over time, depending on how lovers feel, how they treat each other and whether life is stressful or not.

You can be grateful that God's love is very different. First, John tells you that God is the source of love (1 John 4:7). Unlike earthly affection, His love does not fluctuate. The Father does not care for you more if you have pleased him or less if you have failed or sinned.

Jesus Christ surrendered His life on the Cross so that you could live eternal life and enjoy fellowship with God while you still live on earth. The motivation of Jesus was love for humanity.

Father, thank You for the amazing love that You extend to me. Forgive me for not believing the truth about who you are. I pray for a life-changing revelation of Your affection for me, so that I could relate to You and others in a new way. Amen.

Lord guide me.

_____
_____
_____
_____
_____
_____
_____
_____
_____
_____

Lord Teach me to:

_____
_____
_____
_____
_____
_____
_____
_____

Today I am thankful for:

_____
_____
_____
_____
_____
_____
_____
_____

Day 24

"For God has not given us the spirit of fear, but of power, love, and sound mind."
2 Timothy 1:7.

There is fear that comes with living as a black man. There are several black men who are brutalized on different accounts every day, and no one cares or worries about them.

This alone can cause fear to a black man. God, however, has not given us the spirit of fear. God says you are not timid, forget the fears that society has unconsciously filled your heart, but focus on God's saving grace.

Jesus Himself warned us that we would suffer tribulations and trials in this world. He also urged us to remember that He conquered the world, because He who is in us is greater than he who is in the world.

Dear God, I understand problems that express and aggravate fear every day, problems that are disheartening and do not refer to a man's life. And talk less of a black man. Oh God, You confirm that there is a spirit of power, love and sound mind in me. I release and use these wonderful spirits effectively and exhale doubt. Amen.

Lord guide me.

Lord Teach me to:

Today I am thankful for:

BEAUTY FOR ASHES

Day 25

"And provide for those who grieve in Zion to bestow on them a crown of beauty instead of ashes and the oil of gladness instead of mourning."
Isaiah 61:3.

Regardless of the comfort, joy and happiness that reside in Zion, God knows that there are those who still grieve in Zion, of whom a black man is inclusive.

However, he did not stop there; he explicitly stated that for as many who grieve in Zion, he will give them a crown of beauty in the place of ashes and give them the oil of gladness in the place of mourning.

Just look at the text above and see what God has in store for you. Aren't you amazed that you're part of his agenda? Your rejoicing is now, and nothing stops it.

Dear God, I understand your wonderful promises for me as a black man in the text above makes me elated. Knowing that I am in your plan fills me with Joy. Oh, God, regardless of what I go through, help me know, it's for a moment, and for a season. Amen.

Lord guide me.

_____
_____
_____
_____
_____
_____
_____
_____
_____
_____
_____

Lord Teach me to:

_____
_____
_____
_____
_____
_____
_____
_____
_____
_____

Today I am thankful for:

_____
_____
_____
_____
_____
_____
_____
_____
_____

"Instead of your shame, you will receive a double portion, and instead of disgrace, you will rejoice in your inheritance. And so you will inherit a double portion in your land, and everlasting joy will be yours."
Isaiah 61:7.

Shame, shame is an understatement of what a black man is going through, because there is no security for his life. He can be prosecuted, suffer from racial discrimination, and imprisoned.

Astonishingly, no one listens to his part of the story, because it is believed that he is always wrong, so why listen to his part? Nevertheless, what men say is not what God says. God says today for your shame, I will give you a double.

A double what? Double honor, double joy, double prosperity. God says, I know you have gone through a lot, but it will not stop there. I'll bless you a lot.

Heavenly Father, your word says in the place of my disgrace, I will rejoice in your inheritance, and yes, my joy and confidence are restored. Dear God, I pray this word of yours finds enough faith in me and finds a full reflection from within me until it becomes who I am. Amen.

Lord guide me.

_____
_____
_____
_____
_____
_____
_____
_____
_____
_____

Lord Teach me to:

_____
_____
_____
_____
_____
_____
_____
_____
_____

Today I am thankful for:

_____
_____
_____
_____
_____
_____
_____
_____

A LIGHT TO MANY

Day 27

"Arise, shine, for your light has come, and the glory of the Lord rises upon you."
Isaiah 60:1.

You are light, and light must shine, so if a light is not shining, there is a problem. You have a lot to shine; you have your glory to shine; you have your behavior and morals to shine, whether men believe you are morally upright; you have your discipline to shine, and much more.

God has called us not to please men, but to please him. So what a man thinks of your skin color should not leave you unconcerned to the light of God in you.

He created you with bright light in you, and if you use it, it becomes brighter and brighter, that the systems of this world cannot dim it. It is also empowering, because when you arise, you gain confidence and can see further.

Blessed Redeemer, help me shine this light in me to the ends of the earth, let the light bless lives, touch lives and change lives. Make my light never dim and make me unashamedly proud of the light you have deposited in me. Amen.

Lord guide me.

_____
_____
_____
_____
_____
_____
_____
_____
_____
_____

Lord Teach me to:

_____
_____
_____
_____
_____
_____
_____
_____
_____

Today I am thankful for:

_____
_____
_____
_____
_____
_____
_____
_____

YOUR LABORS ARE GREATLY REWARDED

Day 28

"Always give yourselves fully to the work of the Lord, because you know that your labor in the Lord is not in vain."
1 Corinthians 15:58.

◆◇◆

It can tire and discourage you when you work hard, and all you get in return is a peanut or nothing. This is one of the many situations in which a black man finds himself. But God says that your labors will be greatly rewarded.

Always strive to improve your obedience to Scripture, as evidenced by what you do and how you act in your life, so that you can become more and more like Christ. He says your work in the Lord is not in vain, which means you are toiling in his vineyard and in your endeavors.

Everything we do in His name gives glory and honor to Him, who died and rose again, which gives us the promise of eternal life. That is the reward! That is the "pay" that we receive for our labor in God's vineyard.

Dear Lord, I am glad that my work in the vineyard of the Lord is not in vain. I am glad they are not only rewarded, but also greatly rewarded. Help me know this truth in your infinite mercy. When it looks like I'm tired, I will remember that there's a reward. Amen.

Lord guide me.

Lord Teach me to:

Today I am thankful for:

Day 29

"Yet it shall not be so among you; but whoever desires to become great among you, let him be your servant."
Matthew 20:26.

A wonderful leadership character is a character of God; it was his exquisite leadership that made him gave his only son to die for our sins. And as a black man, you are assigned to his son, and you have to lead like him.

The prerequisite for being an outstanding leader in our Bible text for today is to be a servant. In order to lead effectively, you have to reduce yourself to the position of a servant, to familiarize yourself with the struggles and pain that come with being a servant, as Jesus did. To lead, you have to serve.

Jesus' concept of greatness of service is humility. To serve others, not oneself, to be the last, so that others can be served first. Our love of God is inseparable with our love of our neighbor.

Oh God, I desire to lead effectively, to lead in my home, family, and even in my workplace right and effectively. Assist me, oh God, teach me to be a good leader, help me serve in places I need to, and don't let the benefits of being a leader get me carried away, rather help me lead effectively and to the ultimate. Amen.

Lord guide me.

Lord Teach me to:

Today I am thankful for:

Day 30

"And just as you want men to do to you, you also do to them likewise."
Luke 6:31.

In most cases, black men are carried away by the pain, shame, trials and tribulations they go through as black men. And it is easier to criticize others, but you have to be a true reflection of yourself. You must be an example, both in words and in actions.

Your life must convey a powerful message to others, not just by saying, but also by doing, and in this way, you position yourself better in the world. Treating others in the way you want them to treat you is a Christian principle rooted in godly love, which is poured into your heart from above, and God's love never fails.

This demonstrates the type of love that comes to you only from your Father in heaven when you walk in spirit and truth and remain in full communion with your Heavenly Father.

Dear God, I want to be a better person, I want to see a better world, and I know well that there is a level of responsibility assigned to me. Help me to be the change I want to see, help me lead by example. Amen.

Lord guide me.

_____
_____
_____
_____
_____
_____
_____
_____
_____
_____

Lord Teach me to:

_____
_____
_____
_____
_____
_____
_____
_____
_____

Today I am thankful for:

_____
_____
_____
_____
_____
_____
_____
_____

SELFLESSNESS IN CONDUCTS

"Let nothing be done through selfish ambition or conceit, but in lowliness of mind, let each esteem others better than himself. Let each of you look out not only for his own interests, but also for the interests of others."
Philippians 2:3-4.

In this contemporary society, it is easy to be selfish because it seems to be the normal trend. Having in abundance is not bad, but hoarding everything at the expense of others, which leads to waste when many people need the same thing.

As black men, you have been victims of a selfish society with different selfish leaders, but here God admonishes you to be concerned about the well-being of others. Be selfless, do not follow the negative trend of hoarding things to yourself, do not.

Don't think only of your own interests, but show concern with the interests of those around you. It turns people off you and causes them to avoid you when all you can talk about is your interest.

God, I want to esteem others better than I do for myself, but that seems impossible. I ask for the spirit of selflessness to seek for others, their interests and esteem others more than I do for myself. Amen.

Lord guide me.

_____
_____
_____
_____
_____
_____
_____
_____
_____
_____

Lord Teach me to:

_____
_____
_____
_____
_____
_____
_____
_____
_____
_____

Today I am thankful for:

_____
_____
_____
_____
_____
_____
_____

Day 32

Those who live according to the flesh have their minds set on what the flesh desires; but those who live in accordance with the Spirit have their minds set on what the Spirit desires.
Romans 8:5.

The right mindset will shape the world much more than it is now. The reason the black man was the recipient of several outrageous issues is that many lack the right mindset. The right mindset will shape society and do much more good than harm.

We want to put our fellow men in a tight corner due to their race, skin color, ethnic group, and tribe. This is life in the flesh, which is based on selfish desires and needs.

He wants our mindset renewed, not to focus on things of the flesh, but on things of the spirit. We should focus on things of God. This scripture reminds us that the way in which we live reflects the place in which we have set our thoughts and minds.

Oh Lord, I want my mindset to be renewed. I ask you to clarify my thoughts. That you bring me where what bothers you is what bothers me, and I am not just a speaker or hearer of your word, but one who adequately uses it in thoughts and actions. Amen.

Lord guide me.

Lord Teach me to:

Today I am thankful for:

Day 33

"Do you see someone skilled in their work? They will serve before kings; they will not serve before officials of low rank."
Proverbs 22:29.

Skills are becoming rare these days of technological advances and industrialism. In any work, God has called you to, or at least has given you to do, seek to do it to the best of your ability, to the glory of God.

Hard work works! The diligent man will be promoted above average and inferior men to mingle with the prosperous and successful. Education is only a tool. Intelligence has minimal value. Diligence is the key to hard and persistent effort in fulfilling one's professional duties.

There is no question whether hard work will make you successful or not. This is neither a suggestion nor a possible method of improving professional course. God's word declares it, and that settles it.

Lord God, guide me in excellent work, so that your light can shine before men, and they can glorify you, the only true God I serve. Help me honor you with everything I do in my workplace, from my tasks to the way I talk to people to the respect I give my boss. Amen.

Lord guide me.

Lord Teach me to:

Today I am thankful for:

CULTIVATE GRATITUDE

Day 34

"I will give thanks to you, Lord, with all my heart; I will tell of all your wonderful deeds."
Psalm 9:1.

A grateful heart is a blessed heart. To be grateful means to be in awe of what the Lord has done for you, and to refer to him for his glorious deeds. As a black man, you sometimes feel there is nothing to be grateful for, because situations are not in your favor.

Nothing seems to go well with you, and so what's there to rejoice about. Even if God seems silent and there's nothing you can point to now as his good deed toward you, you still have to thank him.

Develop the heart of gratitude. It pays to be grateful. We love and serve a merciful, gracious Father, and we do not deserve the love, grace and mercy that he lavishes so freely on us. What else could we do, but give him endless thanks and praise in return?

Dear Lord, thank you for the grace that you offer moment by moment and day by day. I pray that you would develop in me a true attitude of gratitude and a heart that recognizes the long-suffering way in which you work in so many areas of my life. Amen.

Lord guide me.

_____
_____
_____
_____
_____
_____
_____
_____
_____
_____
_____

Lord Teach me to:

_____
_____
_____
_____
_____
_____
_____
_____

Today I am thankful for:

_____
_____
_____
_____
_____
_____
_____

FORGIVE DAILY

Day 35

Repay no one evil for evil, but give thought to do what is honorable in the sight of all.
Romans 12:17.

To forgive someone might sound simple. It's tough with the flesh, but with God, it comes in handy. Because you would remember vividly that if God hadn't forgiven you, you wouldn't have been redeemed, you would have been wasted.

Instead, God came through, forgave you, and still forgiving you, how much more you, to your fellow brethren. It might not be easy for a black man to forgive, because you have so many hurts and pains in you. Hand them over to God, ease the burden and forgive.

The more you understand God's grace, the more likely you are to extend grace when you are wronged. The more you internalize God's faithfulness, righteousness and truthfulness, the more these principles will be evident in your life.

Dear God, the flesh reminds me of my weakness, tells me I can retaliate, and makes him feel the pains I felt. But I've come, oh God, to lay all at your feet, to seek for grace to forgive adequately, and even before I get offended, I already forgave. Amen.

Lord guide me.

Lord Teach me to:

Today I am thankful for:

Day 36

You shall love the Lord, your God with all your heart, with all your soul, and with all your might.
Deuteronomy 6:5.

A life that gives Glory to the Lord is a life that loves the Lord. A life that loves the Lord is a life that follows the commandments of the Lord. Giving glory to the Lord is to lift his banner. Only when we are filled with His supernatural love from above can we return this love.

You must also know that God is not concerned with your skin color. He created you, and he desires all His creations to give glory, and you are inclusive.

Only in the power of Christ can we love the Lord, our God, with all our hearts. The more we receive Him, the deeper our love for Him becomes.

Father, let my life glorify you in spirit, thoughts and action. Not once, oh God, will my life derail in glorifying you. God's grace gives me a life of glory to the Lord. Amen.

Lord guide me.

Lord Teach me to:

Today I am thankful for:

KEEP YOUR WORD

But most of all, my brothers and sisters, never take an oath,
by heaven or earth or anything else. Just say a simple
yes or no, so that you will not sin
and be condemned.
James 5:12.

Your speech represents your spiritual state, so you should prioritize integrity in communication. Be a trustworthy man, so nobody asks you to swear.

If you swear by anything in God's province, you bring God into the deal. Some people use God as a front for their falsification. That makes their lie more impressive to the unwary. When we make an opinion and present it as truth, we lie.

Now, when a man is a liar, he often swears constantly that he is telling the truth. That is why you should be suspicious of the person who constantly says, "Oh, this is God's honest truth man."

Lord, I thank You, because you are always true to your word. You love those who always speak the truth, and you hate a lying tongue. I want to be truthful always, and I want people to confide in me and bring glory to your name, Lord. Amen.

Lord guide me.

Lord Teach me to:

Today I am thankful for:

Day 38

Know this; my beloved brothers let every person be quick to hear, slow to speak, slow to anger; for the anger of man does not produce the righteousness of God.
James 1:19-20.

Anger is a tool that the devil uses to talk about people, especially black men. Moreover, an average person already believes a black man is an angry man, but that's not true.

Over time, however, we have allowed our experiences to mold us, and we transfer aggression and get angry about little things. The scripture records that anger rests in the bosom of fools. Ecclesiastes 7:9.

Too often in life, we discover the folly of opening our mouths and reacting in careless haste to the words and actions of others. Too often we react in annoyance or anger, only to discover that we misunderstood the facts of the matter, which made us regret that we spoke so quickly and acted so hastily.

God, I see many reasons to be angry; I renounce and resist the spirit of anger within me through your help and spirit. In the place of anger, I receive unspeakable joy. Amen.

Lord guide me.

Lord Teach me to:

Today I am thankful for:

Whoever walks with the wise becomes wise, but the companion of fools will suffer harm.
Proverbs 13:20.

If a black man has the privilege of being in the company or circle of right personalities, it is one of the best blessings on earth. When a man walks in the right company, he enjoys the support of many. This can come as spiritual help, advice, counseling, financially and what have you.

Here is one of the most valuable proverbs for your advancement. The biblical term "walk" means "to go with." It refers to following a certain lifestyle, of conduction in a certain way.

Though you may be wise, foolish friends will eventually destroy you. Though you may be foolish, wise friends will show and teach you success. This is an easy way to prosper. You are the company you keep.

Dear God, I ask in your infinite mercy that you send the right personalities my way. Surround me with the right people, oh God, not the ones who will be envious of the steps and decisions I make, but the ones I can grow and succeed together with. Amen.

Lord guide me.

_____
_____
_____
_____
_____
_____
_____
_____
_____
_____
_____

Lord Teach me to:

_____
_____
_____
_____
_____
_____
_____
_____
_____

Today I am thankful for:

_____
_____
_____
_____
_____
_____
_____
_____

BE A MENTOR TO OTHERS

Day 40

*Instruct the wise, and they will be even wiser. Teach the
righteous, and they will learn even more.*
Proverbs 9:9.

It is not only enough to learn a lot, but also to have someone
who benefits from you. As a black man, you have to deliberately
seek someone to give those lessons to. You too need someone to
point you in the right direction and encourage you on the way.

You also have to do it for someone else. There are no hard and
fast rules to this. You have to think about what will build trust
and help your relationship develop in the way you think it needs
to.

When a young man can meet an adult who was like him in many
ways as a teenager and has become a successful, productive
citizen, it becomes clear to the young man he could do well as an
adult.

Oh, God, there are many young black men who are making several
mistakes. I sincerely hope we could lead these little ones, teach
them, and guide them in the right direction. Oh, God, help me,
help several other black men, so that we can be a blessing for these
young people and raise a generation with the right mindset. Amen.

80

Lord guide me.

Lord Teach me to:

Today I am thankful for:

DEVELOP PATIENCE

Since God chose you to be the holy people he loves, you must clothe yourselves with tenderhearted mercy, kindness, humility, gentleness, and patience.
Colossians 3:12.

On any given day, you may encounter frustrating people and situations, such as a mischievous child, uncooperative coworker, or slow commute. You may feel like lashing out, but God wants you to remain calm and be patient with everyone. Proverbs 15:18.

You should strive for such composure. Secondly, you should recognize how harmful impatience is. It can hurt others and close dialogue. Responding calmly gives people room to confess wrongdoing, explain their attitudes, and make changes.

When you rely on the Holy Spirit, He empowers you to wade through moments of waiting and provocation without being agitated. A calm demeanor in times of delay or adversity can be a powerful witness to God's transforming work.

Lord, I pray for patience and understanding in all areas of my life. Let patience have its way with my heart, so that I can reflect a God-like patience to those around me. Amen.

Lord guide me.

Lord Teach me to:

Today I am thankful for:

JESUS CHRIST THE GREATEST

Day 42

"To open their eyes and turn them from darkness to light,
and from the power of Satan to God, so that they may
receive forgiveness of sins and a place among those
who are sanctified by faith in me."
Acts 26:18.

The more you praise Jesus, the greater He will be in your eyes. Jesus said, "I am the Light of the World" (John 8:12). We are always told to trust God and have faith in Him. This is easier said than done in certain situations.

Do you wander in a spiritual darkness and follow a blind religious guide after another? Jesus is the only light you need to lead you into the holy presence of God. By trusting in Christ, you become a son of God.

When you are sanctified to God, you move from the place of darkness to light; you move from the power of Satan to God; you move from doubt to conviction.

My Lord, My Savior, My King, Your greatness cannot be denied, it cannot be contested, and there is no one greater. Thank you for your faithfulness and unconditional love. You are indeed great, Majestic and Awesome. There's none like you. Amen.

Lord guide me.

Lord Teach me to:

Today I am thankful for:

Day 43

But seek first the kingdom of God and His righteousness, and all these things shall be added to you.
Matthew 6:33.

Instead of seeking the things of this world first, you are urged to seek Him first to develop a right perspective, to exchange natural thinking with Godly thinking.

You have to trust Him to fulfill his promise to meet your needs, remembering that He can do much more beyond what you ask or think. Ephesians 3:20. Take the words of Jesus to the heart to seek Him first, and make Him your focus today and daily.

God knows that fear entraps the heart, and fear fractures faith, which can lead to a spiral into a pit of despair. He also knows you have daily needs, and He has given many precious promises throughout Scripture that He will be your Provider for all the needs and necessities of life if you trust Him.

Loving Father, I know that too often insufficient faith in Your promises of provision has led me to seek for the things of this world by myself. I confess this is a lack of faith in you, and pray the eyes of my heart will be focused on you from this day on. In Jesus' name, I pray. Amen.

Lord guide me.

_____
_____
_____
_____
_____
_____
_____
_____
_____

Lord Teach me to:

_____
_____
_____
_____
_____
_____
_____
_____

Today I am thankful for:

_____
_____
_____
_____
_____
_____

Day 44

"When anxiety was great within me, your consolation brought joy to my soul."
Psalm 94:19.

In many cases, an average person is anxious and worried about various things. What about a black man? He gets worried about many things, virtually everything.

The black man is, by default, an anxious or worried man in the segregation society in which he finds himself. God says there is joy and consolation in the place of worry. God is not only exceptional in the healing of physical illnesses, as many believe, but also an expert in dealing with emotional challenges.

You can live a life without anxieties and worries, if only you'll let God have his way. From the verse, you can see that when you feel worried, God is your only reliance, and that only God can make you from worried to happy.

Dear God, I ask you to heal me from fears and worries according to your loving mercies and kindness. Help me trust you. Know well that everything left in your care does not fail or destroy. Amen.

Lord guide me.

Lord Teach me to:

Today I am thankful for:

Day 45

*I will worship toward thy holy temple, and praise thy name
for thy loving-kindness and for thy truth: for thou hast
magnified thy word above all thy name.*
Psalm 138:2.

Worshiping the Lord will fill your heart with joy and bring you
into His presence, so that you can run on His strength, not your
own. Praise is an invitation to the Holy Spirit to come and dwell
in you. Praises honor the Lord for who he is.

Praise-filled life is a daily exercise designed by God to lift you
above your circumstances, raise you above life challenges, give
you true joy, and give healing in the midst of pain.

If you are faced with serious concerns, you should praise the
Lord. It may sound crazy, but it works. You may not feel like it,
simply do it from your heart anyway. You praise him for his
loving-kindness and truth in his promises.

Father, thank You for the gift of praise today. Thank you for
revealing yourself to me through Your Word, Your Spirit and Your
Creation, that I could stand in awe of You alone. You are worthy of
praise and glory and honor. Amen.

Lord guide me.

Lord Teach me to:

Today I am thankful for:

Day 46

A gentle answer deflects anger, but harsh words make temper flare. 2 The tongue of the wise makes knowledge appealing, but the mouth of a fool belches out foolishness.
Proverbs 15:1-2.

Gentle speech can sometimes be so difficult to find, especially in the conversation of a black man, courtesy of the society that raised him. A black man can speak gentle words. The words you speak and the messages from your lips should be spoken in spirit, in truth, in grace, and in love.

You go into several arguments to prove a point; you don't always have to prove a point in your debate. They create quarrels, hate speech, which leads to malice, and much more.

Words can be helpful and healing. They can give hope and encouragement. Wise and gracious words are a powerful tool in "pouring oil into troubled waters" or dispelling a situation that could quickly escalate into a serious conflict.

Dear God, you are slow to speak and quick to listen. Give me your meek attitude. Restrain me from my speech and conversations. Teach me when to be silent and when to speak. Teach me, Oh Lord, for it is your instructions on which I rely solely. Amen.

Lord guide me.

Lord Teach me to:

Today I am thankful for:

Day 47

"So you are no longer a slave, but God's child; and since you are his child, God has made you also an heir."
Galatians 4:7.

The Scripture says, "I no longer call you slaves, for the slave does not know what his master does, but I call you friend." How deliberately, a black man, the kingdom, and the system of this world look down on and belittle, a generation God calls his friend? You are not a slave.

A son is both rich and the heir of his father's inheritance because of his close family ties, while a slave is poor and is denied any right of succession or part of the son's heritage.

If you have trusted Christ on the side of Calvary's resurrection, you will have all the riches of His grace available to you, not for your godliness, but because of Christ's sacrifice on the cross.

Dear God, thank You, that I am no longer a slave. Thank You, oh God, I am not worthy of being called neither Your son nor Your friend, but You have established this truth with ease. I pray that I can live as a dutiful son who only does the things that honor You. In the name of Jesus, I pray, Amen.

Lord guide me.

_____
_____
_____
_____
_____
_____
_____
_____
_____
_____

Lord Teach me to:

_____
_____
_____
_____
_____
_____
_____
_____

Today I am thankful for:

_____
_____
_____
_____
_____
_____
_____

NO MORE TEARS

Day 48

"He will wipe every tear from their eyes. There will be no more death, mourning, crying or pain, for the old order of things has passed away."
Revelation 21:4.

Tears can be in two forms, it could be tears of joy or sadness, but here we will consider the tears that come with sadness. When a black man is unable to fulfill his duties, as he should, he tears or weeps.

Because society stereotypically raises a male child to toughen up and shows no signs of weakness, he goes into the secret to shed those tears alone.

God Himself will dry every tear, for He enters every searing pain and every aching heart. Not a secret sigh that crosses the portals of your mind, nor a stabbing pain that cuts deep into your hurting heart is missed by your gracious God of love. He is your great God of comfort and Lord of life.

Father, I know that you are the one who holds the future, and I trust my life in your hands today, knowing that you are with me in every trial and every pain I face. I don't understand, but I trust in your loving kindness and tenderness. Amen.

Lord guide me.

Lord Teach me to:

Today I am thankful for:

MORE THAN A CONQUEROR

Day 49

"Yet in all things, we are more than conquerors through Him who loved us."
Romans 8:37.

There are overwhelming battles for a black man then and now. The battle of his identity to the battle of abusive rules that attack his personality every day. Some battles are finances, others are racial, family, society, etc. The scripture confirms that you are more than a conqueror.

The Scripture did not say that you are a conqueror. It was said that you are more than a conqueror. Nothing is impossible with God. Believe in His Word, which says: in all these things, you are more than conqueror by Him, who loves you.

This is a godly principle of faith that, when you abide in Christ in the inevitable disasters that flood your life, faith increases, trust increases, hope increases, and your love of Jesus reaches even greater heights.

Dear God, affirmatively through your power of conviction, I decree I am more than a conqueror. In my career, I'm more than a conqueror, in my finances, I'm more than a conqueror, in all facets of my life, I'm more than a conqueror through him that loved me. Amen.

98

Lord guide me.

Lord Teach me to:

Today I am thankful for:

VICTORY IS YOURS

Day 50

"These things I have spoken unto you, that in me you might have peace." In the world, you shall have tribulation: but be of good cheer; I have overcome the world."
John 16:33.

Sometimes the assurance of victory for a black man looks bleak and impossible, because he sees several other black men struggling through this path and dying along the way. Too bad, this has unconsciously shaped the thoughts of the black man.

As he strives to be better daily, he already has a residual thought that one of those days he will no longer be. Just know that Christ has won the victory on your behalf, so that you are safe in the arms of Jesus, no matter what happens.

The incarnate WORD of God has given you a clear message that He has gained victory over Satan and this world system. He has given you a glimpse of the wonderful things God has prepared for those who love Him.

Dear Father, thank you for Your wonderful words of comfort and peace. Oh, God, of divine victory, every tinge of victory belongs to you, help me be victorious. I pray that His perfect peace will bring me through all life's difficulties, to Your praise and glory. Amen

Lord guide me.

_____
_____
_____
_____
_____
_____
_____
_____
_____
_____
_____

Lord Teach me to:

_____
_____
_____
_____
_____
_____
_____
_____
_____
_____

Today I am thankful for:

_____
_____
_____
_____
_____
_____
_____
_____
_____

CONCLUSION

Dear reader, I sincerely hope this book was an encouragement to you, and that God has touched your heart. If you have not yet accepted Jesus Christ as Your Lord and Savior, I invite you to do so now. Also, maybe you have lost your way and would like to rededicate your life to Jesus. I encourage you to repeat the sinner's prayer.

Heavenly Father, it is written in Your Word that if I confess with my mouth that Jesus is Lord and believe in my heart that You have raised Him from the dead, I shall be saved. Therefore, Father, I confess Jesus is my Lord. I make Him the Lord of my life right now. I believe in my heart that you raised Jesus from the dead. I renounce my past life with Satan and close the door to any of his devices. I thank You for forgiving me of all my sins. Jesus is my Lord, and I am a new creation. Old things have passed away. Now all things have become new in Jesus' name. Amen.

Romans 10:9

That if thou shalt confess with thy mouth the Lord Jesus, and shalt believe in thine heart that God hath raised him from the dead, thou shalt be saved.

Made in the USA
Columbia, SC
14 November 2024

46514805R00059